peggy fleming

by Charles and Ann Morse

illustrated by Harold Henriksen

CREATIVE EDUCATION
MANKATO, MINNESOTA

Published by Creative Education, 123 South Broad Street, P. O. Box 227,
Mankato, Minnesota 56001
Copyright © 1974 by Creative Education. International copyrights reserved in all countries.
No part of this book may be reproduced in any form without written permission
from the publisher. Printed in the United States.
Distributed by Childrens Press, 1224 West Van Buren Street, Chicago, Illinois 60607
Library of Congress Numbers 74-18429   ISBN: 0-87191-380-1
Cover: Sports Illustrated photo by John G. Zimmerman © Time, Inc.

Library of Congress Cataloging in Publication Data
Morse, Charles.   Peggy Fleming.
SUMMARY: A biography of the figure skater who went from winning two
consecutive world championships in 1966 and 1967 to being the only Olympic
gold medal winner for the United States in the 1968 winter games.
1. Fleming, Peggy—Juvenile literature. 2. Skating—Juvenile literature.
(1. Fleming, Peggy, 2. Ice skating—Biography)
I. Morse, Ann, joint author. II. Keely, John, illus. III. Title.
GV850.F55M67   796.9'1'0924 (B) (Fic) 74-18429   ISBN 0-87191-380-1

The glamorous cities of Europe were far from the mind of nine-year-old Peggy Gale Fleming when she laced on a pair of skates for the first time.

"It was amazing," Peggy's older sister Janice recalls, "Peggy took to skating right off." Gliding away from the changing bench without a wobble or a fall, she seemed made for skating.

Peggy Fleming began her skating career that Sunday afternoon in 1957 in Cleveland, Ohio. She continued it through long years of practice and determination. Finally she tested it far from the Cleveland Arena in the other worlds of Davos, Vienna, and Grenoble.

Before going to Davos, Switzerland, for the world figure-skating championships in 1966, Peggy was already a champion. She had won three United States women's figure skating championships in 1964.

Those victories had brought Peggy to the Winter Olympics at Innsbruck, Austria. There, before a gallery that included members from the Royal House of Orange, Peggy took a gigantic fall and finished in sixth place.

The following year, the 1965 world figure-skating championships were held in Colorado Springs. The altitude in Colorado Springs presented problems for 16-year-old Peggy.

Her family lived in Pasadena, California, which is nearer sea level. The pull of gravity at a low altitude puts more strain on the muscles. Peggy was, therefore, practicing only about an hour a day. As a result, she tired quickly in the competition at Colorado Springs and finished third. A Canadian and an Austrian finished ahead of her.

Soon after the 1965 world championships, the Flemings moved to Colorado Springs. Peggy's father, Albert, was a printer and his job required that he move often. In fact, the Flemings had moved so frequently around the United States and Canada that it was difficult for Peggy to keep all the years and places straight.

The move to Colorado Springs, however, was different. This time the family moved for Peggy's sake. At the higher altitude, Peggy's energy was not so quickly drained. She was able to practice many hours each day. The family lived near the Broadmoor Hotel Ice School where Peggy was coached by Carlo Fassi.

Peggy's loss in the 1965 championships had disappointed people all over the United States. It had been five years since the U.S. could boast of a winner in figure skating. The 1960's had begun with tragedy for skating. On February 15, 1961, the news flash from Belgium read: "A Sabena Airlines Boeing 707 crashed near the Brussels Airport early today, killing 73 persons, including the 18 members of the United States figure-skating team."

The nation's top skaters and figure-skating teachers were all dead.

Figure-skating fans began to fear in 1965 that the whole decade would go by without one United States winner. For a nation that had won 21 world figure-skating championships in 13 years before the crash and not one since, it was a disappointing outlook.

At the beginning of 1966, sports writers pinned all their hopes on Peggy. The quiet, 5-foot, 3½-inch, 108-pound skater had just won the U.S. Senior Ladies' figure-skating title for the third straight year. Everyone wondered if 17-year-old Peggy Fleming was prepared to take on the world.

Since the move to Colorado Springs, Peggy had determined she would be ready for the 1966 championships. Like most young skating champions, Peggy was up at dawn and skated from 6 a.m. to 11 a.m. After her classes at Cheyenne Mountain School, there was more practice from 5 p.m. to 8 p.m. Peggy kept her social life to a minimum. There were very, very few late nights.

The Fleming family also had their share of sacrifices as they all helped Peggy to keep moving toward her goal — a world championship. Sometimes it was difficult for Peggy's three sisters because so much attention was given to Peggy. Still, each of the daughters was encouraged to develop her own skills.

Janice Fleming was given the support she needed to pursue a nursing career. Maxine, three years younger than Peggy, followed an interest in fashion while in college. Cathy, six years younger than Peggy, loves to skate, but "just for fun." She has never felt that she had to compete with Peggy.

Though the Flemings moved often, the girls made friends easily. The Fleming house soon became a gathering place for the girls and their friends. Their projects included sewing their own clothes. They also worked in the art studio in their garage. "Home is where the fun is," Peggy once said.

Home was also where the work was. At home in Colorado Springs Peggy spent thousands of hours working on school figures. School figures are geometrical designs traced by the skater on the ice. The simplest of these patterns is the figure eight. Peggy had to learn 70 figures, all based on the fundamental figure eight, in order to pass the United States Figure-Skating Association (USFSA) official tests.

The idea behind a figure eight is to skate a circle on one foot and come back to the starting place. Then the skater traces another circle on the other foot, once more returning to the starting point. On clean ice, the skate blade leaves a white mark. That mark or "trace" is a drawing. It has to be made carefully and exactly.

It takes a great deal of understanding and body control to transcribe the compulsory figures onto the ice. Since Peggy's main weakness was always in tracing accurate figures, she spent long and tedious hours practicing them in preparation for the 1966 world championships.

Peggy practiced the figures until she could do each one to perfection. This included making each circle's diameter three times the height of the skater. It is not enough

to skate a perfect figure only once. Peggy learned to repeat a figure, tracing it so that each line fitted right on top of the preceding ones.

Early in March, it was time to travel to Switzerland. Peggy arrived in prime form. She had skated five hours a day, six days a week for a year. The altitude at Davos was the same as at Colorado Springs. Coach Carlo Fassi made sure Peggy was prepared for the high altitude and cold weather by having West German team trainer Curt Schumacher rub Peggy's legs with liniment each time she skated. When she left the ice, Schumacher would take off the liniment with alcohol so that her legs wouldn't overheat.

Schumacher once said that a skater's biggest fault is that she or he too often goes out cold to skate. Schumacher feels that a skater needs to keep his muscles warm when competing in the cold.

When it came time for the school figure competition, the 5,500-seat stadium at Davos was nearly empty. Compulsory figures are tedious to perform and not much fun to watch.

For almost a week Peggy and her competitors traced and retraced the required figures — counters, rockers, loops, and brackets. They made outside forward eights, inside backward eights, and changes of edge on the ice. The terms used for the figures are as complicated as the maneuvers themselves.

After the skater has cut a figure on the ice and traced it perfectly three times, the judges gather on the ice and study the print. There are at least five judges in figure skating competition. Scoring in skating is complicated. Points from six (perfect) to one (bad) are awarded in both the compulsory figure part of the competition and in free skating.

Skaters make up their own routines for free skating. They perform a variety of jumps, spins, and steps in rhythm to music they have chosen. Judges award two marks in free skating. One is based on technique, the other on composition and style. There are some required free skating maneuvers. These are worth 20 percent of the final scoring. The regular free skating counts 40 percent.

Compulsory figures make up the remaining 40 percent of the skater's final rank. The figures are judged on the manner in which they're skated and on the basis of the tracing left on the ice. Some judges even get down on their hands and knees to view the tracings. They might even use whisk brooms to clear the ice for a better look.

After the compulsory figures and again after the free skating events, the judges each rank all the skaters. The number one is awarded to the skater a judge considers the best. A two goes to the second best and so on. These numbers — one, two, or five or ten — are called ordinals. Generally these numbers or ordinals determine a skater's place in competition. If three of five judges awarded ones to a skater, that skater would be the top one in that event. If the same skater had the most ordinals in the other events, that skater would be the champion.

Peggy flowed through each figure as she skated at Davos. Knowing her movement counted in the judging, she had to keep her body in control and maintain her balance as she executed the figure. Hitches, pulls, or flinches are considered errors. They're also usually reflected in the tracings. Peggy's movements had to be simple and attractive, not strained and affected, if she was to score well.

If she was imperfect in making a figure, Peggy tried to correct it when she retraced. She believed it was better for a skater to show the control necessary to correct a fault instead of repeating that fault.

By the end of that first week in Davos, Peggy was rewarded for spending so much time and effort on the school figures. She led Canada's Petra Burka by a 48-point margin.

U.S. figure-skating officials were ecstatic. "Unless Peggy falls flat on the ice, she's got it in the bag," one member said. But everyone knew such a fall was unlikely for Peggy

Fleming. The young skater excelled in free skating with all its splits and spins and spirals.

However, more people were concerned about Peggy's endurance than they were about Peggy's excellence. Peggy had a bad habit of eating very little. If a restaurant didn't have her favorite dish — macaroni and cheese — she would walk away without eating.

Former Olympic skating champion Dick Button had always given pointers and moral support to Peggy. At Davos he also helped with her diet. He sometimes took Peggy and her mother out to dinner and refused to leave the restaurant until Peggy cleaned her plate.

Reporters at Davos asked Peggy how she felt about her successes, her failures, and the time skating has taken in her life.

Peggy readily admitted that skating is a grinding experience, even grim at times. "There are lots of disappointments," she said somewhat sadly. "Sometimes I fight against being human," Peggy went on to tell an interviewer. "But in overcoming these, I learn; and that makes my life worthwhile."

Going on the ice first in the free skating part of the competition was Petra Burka, Peggy's strongest competitor. The Canadian girl, the defending champion, had problems. At the end of her number she left out two moves.

With a chewing gum wrapper tucked in one glove for good luck, Peggy than glided into the free skating event. Now she had a chance to exhibit her own creation. Accompanied by music, Peggy wove together jumps and spins into a continuous flow.

The small figure in the dark–red skating costume covered the entire ice area with ease, sureness, and rhythm. In an intricate movement called a one-and-a-half, double-cherry-flip combination, Peggy dazzled the spectators in the now jam-packed Davos stadium. Peggy expressed the mood of Tchaikovsky's "Pathetique" as she glided and leaped into an even more difficult spread-eagle, double-axel spread-eagle.

Toward the end of Peggy's routine it looked as though a moment of caution might create a hitch in her perfect performance. But it seemed the judges didn't notice. In fact, one even awarded her a six, the only perfect score to appear in the women's competition. Peggy's lowest mark was a 5.8. Without a hurried or jerky movement, Peggy brought her routine to a close just as the music ended.

It was all over, and Peggy Fleming had become the first American girl to win a world figure-skating championship since Carol Heiss in 1960. Peggy had surprassed defending champion Petra Burka. At last, the United States had found in Peggy Fleming its skater of the decade.

She would go on to even greater glory at Vienna the next year. Before that, Peggy took a victory tour through Austria, Germany, Russia, England, and France. On tour Peggy could relax at last. She could even stay out late. Magazine photographers took pictures of Peggy enjoying springtime in Europe.

World Skating Champion Alain Calmat, whom Peggy first met in Colorado Springs, was her guide around Paris. It was a happy time for Peggy and a relief after eight years of rigid discipline. But her Paris fling ended abruptly when Peggy was notified that her father had died of a heart attack. She returned home, not to the victory celebration Colorado Springs had planned, but to her father's funeral.

Keeping Peggy in shape continued to be a problem for Dick Button. He carried on his eat-more-meat campaign as Peggy practiced for the next world championships at Vienna.

Button has always had a very high regard for Peggy. He once wrote, "She is a skater who has a unique combination of athletic ability, technical control, great style, and immense musicality."

Dick Button was interested in Peggy's maintaining

her strength, but he didn't want to change her style at all. "She is not a fiery skater and she shouldn't be made to .be."

Like many other critics, Button had paid Peggy the very highest praise. "With some skaters there is a lot of fuss and feathers, but nothing is happening. With Peggy there's no fuss and feathers, and a great deal happening."

When Peggy won the 1966 championships, Coach Fassi felt it was Peggy's attitude that made her such a great winner. "She has an excellent disposition," Fassi said after the championships. "It makes her forget a bad practice in 10 minutes. But at the same time she learns from all her mistakes."

Fassi added with pride, "There is no doubt in my mind she is the best in the world."

The year between Davos and Vienna was not easy for Peggy. Her close-knit family had to adjust to the loss of Albert Fleming. High school was over. Peggy was very serious about the studies she was beginning at Colorado College in Colorado Springs.

With her family, her studies, and the future in her mind, she arrived in Vienna in March 1967 to defend her world title.

Vienna, called the birthplace of figure-skating, was

an exciting place. It was even more exciting in 1967 because the Austrians were celebrating the 100th birthday of the Vienna Skating Club.

During the American Civil War, an American dancing master named Jackson Haines had journeyed from the United States to Europe. He used his ballet training to the fullest when he performed on skates. Europeans were overcome by the sheer beauty and flowing ease of his movements.

From Jackson Haines came what is now called the international style, the basis of modern free skating. He founded the skating club in Vienna.

The Austrians cherish their figure-skating history and have won 32 world championships. The Americans have won 23. Each year the competition grows more intense.

Peggy prepared for that first grueling week of school figures. "I have everything to lose," Peggy said softly to her coach at rinkside as she watched the practice of her 22 competitors from 12 countries. A repeat victory might help to nudge Peggy into a lucrative pro career, a goal she had set for herself after her father's death.

Practicing six hours a day, Peggy didn't have to worry as she started into the actual competition. The first of the compulsory figures was an inside counter — a maneuver skated mainly on the inside edges of the blades. Peggy skated the figure right into an eight-point lead over Canada's Valerie Jones and East Germany's Gabriele Seyfert.

At the end of three days and six figures, Peggy led by 69 points. Gabriele's mother moaned, "The best we can hope for now is second place. Peggy is practically unbeatable."

By the end of the compulsory figure competition, Peggy had not only racked up 1,223.4 points, she had achieved a perfect score of nine ordinals. Each of the judges had awarded her first place. This was a milestone in figure-skating history.

Several observers at Vienna noted that Peggy Fleming was the skater without the bruises. Most skaters are covered with battle scars from their practice sessions. Peggy's balance is so keen and her gestures so graceful that she rarely falls.

Peggy is perhaps the only world-class skater who swings gently into a turn. As she does, she picks up momentum by arching her body rather than by springing powerfully off her leg.

Carlo Fassi has never let Peggy over-practice. Yet he has allowed her a great deal of freedom in working out her free skating routines. Peggy leans more toward the ballet-like approach to skating rather than toward the athlet-

ic approach. Actually she tries to combine both approaches, but she feels that the ballet movements work best for her.

Gabriele Seyfert, Peggy's main rival in Vienna, was more athletic in her approach. As she stood at rinkside watching the free-skating finals, she said, "Peggy has no weaknesses. The ideal thing would be to skate as Peggy does, which is softly, and then connect it with high jumps between."

As Peggy glided over the ice to her music, critics and fans noted both approaches. One moment she skated

as gracefully as Bambi, a nickname sportswriters have given her, and the next moment she displayed a more rugged approach.

Then in a flash Peggy fell. She was trying to finish a double axel, a double backward spin. The audience gasped. Peggy was on the seat of her pants, skidding toward the wall.

The tense moment was soon over. While the audience still sat horrified, Peggy was again on her feet dancing fluidly to the music. Her movements were amazingly

delicate as she performed an array of spins, splitzes, and loops.

Finally, Peggy tried another double axel. This time it was perfect. The audience stood and cheered. Amazingly, despite her fall, all the judges named her number one — her second perfect score in the world championships. She had totaled 2,273.4 points, 94 more than Gabriele Seyfert.

For the second year in a row, Peggy was the champion of the world.

"That's nice," Peggy admitted, "but I would like to go out and do the whole thing over again and do it right." When a reporter asked how she could get such power into her leaps, Peggy simply replied, "Inner guts."

The next year would bring the winter Olympics at Grenoble. Could Peggy stay with it? She would ask herself this difficult question over and over again. "This is really a hard sort of life. It's a lot of traveling and training and work and appearances," Peggy told a reporter after the Vienna championships.

People continued to ask Peggy what career she would choose — would she become a professional skater or would she remain an amateur?

Eighteen years old and somewhat confused, Peggy confessed, "Gee, I really look forward to leading a life of my own, a kind of other life. I don't think I will skate in competition too much longer."

It concerned Peggy that her amateur competitions were a great financial drain on her widowed mother. However, an Olympic gold medal could bring Peggy a very profitable professional contract.

In the year between Vienna and Grenoble, Peggy worked more on her ballet approach to skating. Norman Cornick, a dance instructor at Colorado College, tutored Peggy for six hours a week in the art of modern and jazz dancing. Cornick felt that most of the top skaters never seemed really able to dance. But with Peggy, he saw a beautiful flow, "a real feeling for music."

After 10 years and 20,000 hours of labor since that first day of skating at the Cleveland arena, Peggy Fleming headed for Grenoble and the 1968 Winter Olympics.

Doris Fleming, Peggy's mother, watched over her 19-year-old daughter's health in Grenoble. She moved Peggy out of Olympic Village where there was an outbreak of the flu. Peggy and her mother stayed in an old but dignified hideaway hotel. Peggy nursed a sore throat and tried to cover up her nervousness.

But the American figure-skating star didn't really need to worry. At the end of two days of being glared at

by nine judges as she traced rockers and brackets and loops, Peggy completed the compulsory figures with perfect form. She led the Olympic competition by 77.2 points. Gabriele Seyfert was second.

Meanwhile, Mrs. Fleming had been sewing six skating costumes. She and Peggy finally decided on a chartreuse chiffon costume for the free skating event. Grenoble residents liked the costume because chartreuse is the local liqueur and a favorite color.

Of the 32 skaters in the event, Peggy was the 22nd to perform. The audience greeted her warmly. But as one reporter said, "It was the meanest night of her career." The evening was fraught with crises.

Just as Peggy stepped out onto the ice, she caught the rhinestones on her sleeve against her tights. Although she feared the tights would begin to ravel and tear, Peggy glided on, skating to the music.

Peggy was also feeling the pressure of the Olympics. She followed Czechoslovakia's Hana Maskova, a long-legged, graceful person who had just completed a calm, flowing routine. Peggy knew it was a hard act to follow.

When Peggy was only halfway through her routine, she knew she had made many small errors. Her coach had suggested she play it safe with the free skating. But Peggy was determined. She was competing with herself, and she felt she had to do acrobatic leaps and spins. The overall difficulty of a routine is one of the factors graded by judges.

Coach Fassi found he was often afraid to look. He saw some errors and knew that out on the ice Peggy was scared. Yet, when she came off the ice, her artistry had brought her a standing ovation and a total score of 1,970.5 points.

But Peggy was in tears. It was a rougher emotional test than she had expected. It had taken its toll.

The reward was the Olympic gold medal. Peggy finished 88.2 points ahead of Gabriele Seyfert and 141.7 points better than Hana Maskova. The Colorado College coed stepped onto the winner's podium to accept the only Olympic gold medal won by the United States that year.

"This feeling can never be shared," said the young skating champion, "even by the richest people."

Grenoble, Vienna, and Davos — these were three faraway places that ushered a young, amateur skater right into several professional contracts. Each place holds special memories for Peggy. It was in these cities that she became one of America's greatest champions.

After Grenoble, NBC-TV signed Peggy to a long-term contract. All three national ice shows in this country were also eager to sign her. Overnight Peggy had become a professional.

In 1970 Peggy married Gregory Jenkins in Sherman Oaks, California. She and Gregory had met five years earlier when in her spare time Peggy had coached Greg's fraternity hockey team at Colorado College. Though she hadn't felt that the team played hockey or skated very well, she had enjoyed the challenge.

Recently Peggy traveled to a new place for her — Moscow. She went there to do a special television program, "Peggy Fleming Visits the Soviet Union." It was the first American entertainment show filmed entirely in the Soviet Union. The special was televised in both the United States and Russia on the same evening.

While the honors Peggy has won were always satisfying, the people and places stand out most in Peggy's memories. In Leningrad, a Russian gave Peggy a book of Shakespeare's sonnets.

The man told Peggy that he was offering her a little beauty in thanks for all the beauty Peggy had brought to the world.

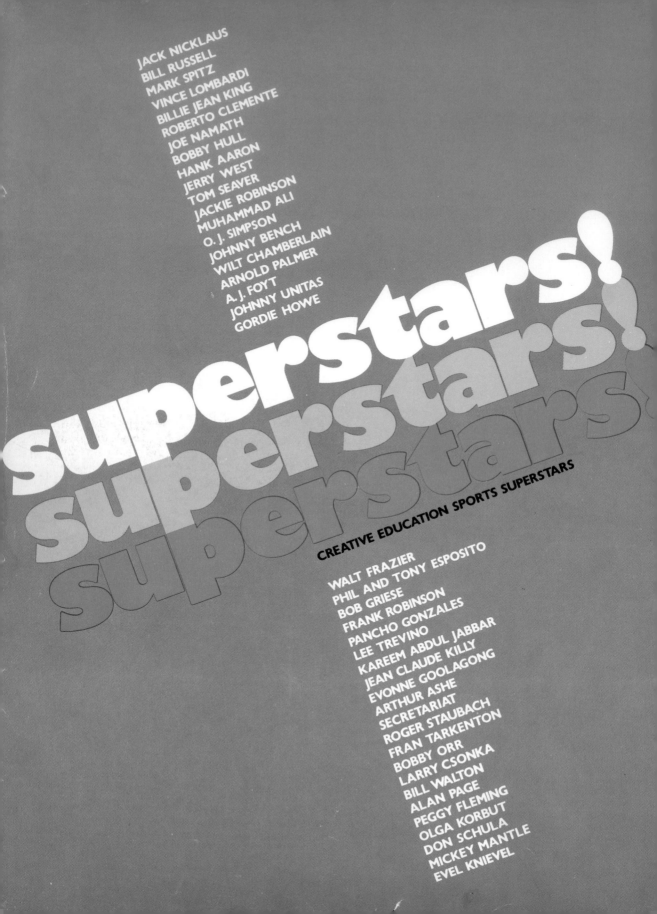

JACK NICKLAUS
BILL RUSSELL
MARK SPITZ
VINCE LOMBARDI
BILLIE JEAN KING
ROBERTO CLEMENTE
JOE NAMATH
BOBBY HULL
HANK AARON
JERRY WEST
TOM SEAVER
JACKIE ROBINSON
MUHAMMAD ALI
O. J. SIMPSON
JOHNNY BENCH
WILT CHAMBERLAIN
ARNOLD PALMER
A. J. FOYT
JOHNNY UNITAS
GORDIE HOWE

superstars!
superstars!
superstars!
superstars!

CREATIVE EDUCATION SPORTS SUPERSTARS

WALT FRAZIER
PHIL AND TONY ESPOSITO
BOB GRIESE
FRANK ROBINSON
PANCHO GONZALES
LEE TREVINO
KAREEM ABDUL JABBAR
JEAN CLAUDE KILLY
EVONNE GOOLAGONG
ARTHUR ASHE
SECRETARIAT
ROGER STAUBACH
FRAN TARKENTON
BOBBY ORR
LARRY CSONKA
BILL WALTON
ALAN PAGE
PEGGY FLEMING
OLGA KORBUT
DON SCHULA
MICKEY MANTLE
EVEL KNIEVEL